Buddhism for Bears

Buddhism for Bears

Illustrated by Chris Riddell

Text by Claire Nielson

ST. MARTIN'S PRESS
New York

Library of Congress Cataloging-in-Publication Data

Nielson, Claire.
     Buddhism for bears / text by Claire Nielson ; illustrated by
Chris Riddell. – 1st U.S. ed.
        p. cm.
     Originally published: London : Ebury Press, 1995.
     ISBN 0-312-20503-1
     1. Buddhism Caricatures and cartoons. 2. Buddhism—
Humor.
     I. Riddell, Chris. II. Title.
BQ4060.N54   1999
294.3'02'07—dc21

                                          99-22785
                                               CIP

First published in Great Britain by Ebury Press, an imprint of
Random House UK Limited

First U.S. Edition: July 1999

10 9 8 7 6 5 4 3 2 1

Contents

Wisdom

Ask yourself, what is power?

Experience life as a flowing movement

Keep in touch with the here and now

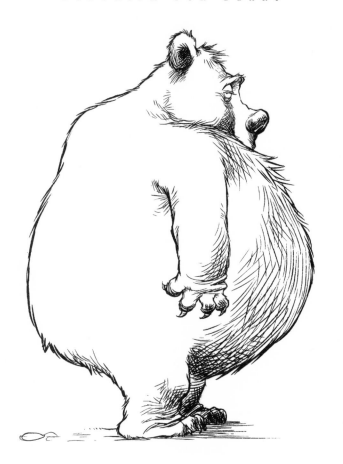

It is unwise to eat to
one's utmost capacity

Endeavour to find the one behind the many

Let go of the craving and greed ...

... that bind you to the world

There are skilled and unskilled states of mind

Love other living beings as members of the universe

Banish interests and activities opposed
to the ideal of enlightenment

Self-Control

Refrain from taking
what has not been given

Avoid the distinctive …

... and the superficial

Abstain from drinking intoxicating liquors and spirits

Abstain from non-celibacy

Even in dreams do not
commit unwholesome
offences

31

Have no use for luxurious beds and seats

Practice self-restraint with regard to your fellow beings

Do not squander energy in the
foolish pursuit of the inconsequential

Techniques

For meditation select a room
that is quiet, clean and tidy

Sitting is the foundation of meditation

Sit with a sense of gratitude and dignity

You may experience the dropping-off of body and mind

Beginners in meditation should not sit for too long a time

The lotus position may hurt the beginner's legs

Always adopt an erect sitting position when meditating

Endeavour to experience each breath you take in and out

Liberate the spirit

Endeavour to make the mind void

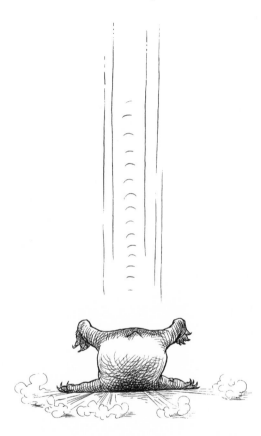

Do not allow your mind to become dull or lax

Choose nourishing vegetables ...

… rather than meat

Vigorous body movements may
evoke a feeling of wellbeing

Seek to govern your behaviour by the
principle of non-violence

Principles of behaviour may be transmitted
from teachers to disciple

Demonstrate a spirit of tenderness towards others

Practice complete awareness of body,
thoughts and feelings

Cultivate a profound silence
in the deepest recesses of the mind

61

Constantly question how to live in the
world and yet find liberation

Truth

At certain points during meditation you will
suddenly have insights about yourself

All is equally holy, be it diamonds or dung

The perfect way knows no difficulties

Demonstrate reality rather than discuss it

The true nature of the void remains unknown

Existence is a never-ending flow of change

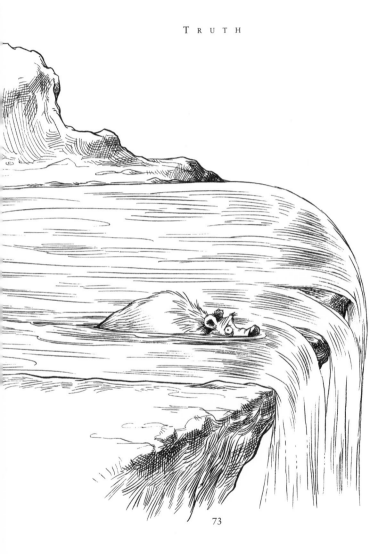

73

The inner being should not
be shackled to the body

Renounce all worldly things

Self-mortification does not lead to inner truth

Be ready for the
great awakening

79

Remember to allow the law
of karma to regulate all activities